MICHIGAN

The Great Lakes State

BY
JOHN HAMILTON

Abdo & Daughters
An imprint of Abdo Publishing | abdopublishing.com

abdopublishing.com

Published by ABDO Publishing, a division of ABDO, PO Box 398166, Minneapolis, Minnesota 55439. Copyright © 2017 by Abdo Consulting Group, Inc. International copyrights reserved in all countries. No part of this book may be reproduced in any form without written permission from the publisher. ABDO & Daughters™ is a trademark and logo of ABDO Publishing.

Printed in the United States of America, North Mankato, Minnesota.
022016
092016

Editor: Sue Hamilton   **Contributing Editor:** Bridget O'Brien
Graphic Design: Sue Hamilton
Cover Art Direction: Candice Keimig   **Cover Photo Selection:** Neil Klinepier
Cover Photo: iStock
Interior Images: Alamy, AP, Baraga County Tourist & Recreation Assoc, Corbis, David Olson, Detroit Lions, Detroit Pistons, Detroit Red Wings, Detroit Tigers, Edmon Low Library/Oklahoma State Univ, Fiat Chrysler Automobiles, Ford Motor Company, Geoff Ingalls, Gerald R. Ford Presidential Museum, Gilmore Car Museum, General Motors/Jeffrey Sauger, Government of Ontario Art Collection, Granger, Gunter Kuchler, History in Full Color-Restoration/Colorization, iStock, Kellogg Company, Library of Congress, Michigan Dept of Transportation, Minden Pictures, Mile High Maps, NY Public Library, Science Source, Univ of Michigan Museum of Natural History, Wayne County Airport Authority/Vito Palmisano, White House, & Wikimedia.

Statistics: *State and City Populations*, U.S. Census Bureau, July 1, 2015/2014 estimates; *Land and Water Area*, U.S. Census Bureau, 2010 Census, MAF/TIGER database; *State Temperature Extremes*, NOAA National Climatic Data Center; *Climatology and Average Annual Precipitation*, NOAA National Climatic Data Center, 1980-2015 statewide averages; *State Highest and Lowest Points*, NOAA National Geodetic Survey.

Websites: To learn more about the United States, visit booklinks.abdopublishing.com. These links are routinely monitored and updated to provide the most current information available.

Cataloging-in-Publication Data

Names: Hamilton, John, 1959- author.
Title: Michigan / by John Hamilton.
Description: Minneapolis, MN : Abdo Publishing, [2017] | Series: The United
    States of America | Includes index.
Identifiers: LCCN 2015957615 | ISBN 9781680783247 (lib. bdg.) |
    ISBN 9781680774283 (ebook)
Subjects: LCSH: Michigan--Juvenile literature.
Classification: DDC 977.4--dc23
LC record available at http://lccn.loc.gov/2015957615

CONTENTS

THE GREAT LAKES STATE

Michigan is thousands of miles from either the Atlantic or Pacific Oceans, and yet it is a boater's paradise. That is because it is nearly surrounded by four of the five Great Lakes. Michigan has more freshwater coastline than any other state. (It also has the most lighthouses!)

Early in Michigan's history, fur traders made fortunes, thanks to the state's lakes and rivers. Today, massive ships carrying millions of tons of iron ore, steel products, coal, grains, and other bulk cargo pass through the busy locks of Sault Ste. Marie and the Straits of Mackinac on their way to industrial centers like Detroit.

Michigan is well known for making cars, and for the soul-pop sound of Detroit's Motown bands. But it is also famous for its natural beauty, from lofty sand dunes and sparkling trout streams to millions of acres of wildlife-filled forests.

A sailboat glides past Holland Harbor Light, better known as "Big Red." It is one of Michigan's most popular lighthouses.

QUICK FACTS

Name: Michigan may come from an Ojibwe Native American word, *mishigama*, which means "great lake."

State Capital: Lansing, population 114,620

Date of Statehood: January 26, 1837 (26th state)

Population: 9,922,576 (10th-most populous state)

Area (Total Land and Water): 96,714 square miles (250,488 sq km), 11th-largest state

Largest City: Detroit, population 680,250

Nickname: The Great Lakes State; The Wolverine State

Motto: *Si quaeris peninsulam amoenam circumspice* (If you seek a pleasant peninsula, look about you)

State Bird: American Robin

State Flower: Apple Blossom

State Rock: Petoskey Stone

State Tree: White Pine

State Song: "My Michigan"

Highest Point: Mount Arvon, 1,979 feet (603 m)

Lowest Point: Lake Erie, 571 feet (174 m)

Average July High Temperature: 80°F (27°C)

Record High Temperature: 112°F (44°C), in Mio and Stanwood on July 13, 1936

Average January Low Temperature: 12°F (-11°C)

Record Low Temperature: -51°F (-46°C), in Vanderbilt on February 9, 1934

Average Annual Precipitation: 33 inches (84 cm)

Number of U.S. Senators: 2

Number of U.S. Representatives: 14

U.S. Postal Service Abbreviation: MI

GEOGRAPHY

Michigan is a state in the Midwest region of the United States. Its total land and water area is 96,714 square miles (250,488 sq km), making it the 11th-largest state. However, almost 40 percent of that is water area. Only 56,539 square miles (146,435 sq km) is land. Michigan has 3,224 miles (5,189 km) of shoreline, including many large islands.

Thousands of years ago, huge Ice Age glaciers repeatedly scoured the land. When they finally melted, the water they left behind created the Great Lakes. They also left behind nearly 11,000 inland lakes in Michigan.

Michigan is split between two large pieces of land called the Lower and Upper Peninsulas. They are each unique, with their own geography and character.

Sand dunes on the Lower Peninsula.

A waterfall on the Upper Peninsula.

Michigan's total land and water area is 96,714 square miles (250,488 sq km). It is the 11th-largest state. The state capital is Lansing.

Michigan's Lower Peninsula is shaped like a big mitten. It shares its southern borders with Indiana and Ohio. To the east are Lake Huron, Lake Erie, and the province of Ontario, Canada. To the west is Lake Michigan. The city of Detroit is the only city in the United States where you can drive south into Canada.

Along with Detroit, most of Michigan's other large cities are in the Lower Peninsula. About 97 percent of the state's people live in this region. Outside of the cities there are many farms. The soil is fertile, especially in the south. The land is mostly flat.

A pumpkin patch near St. Johns, Michigan. Michigan's Lower Peninsula has a great deal of flat, fertile farmland.

The Upper Peninsula is rocky and hilly. The people here are often called "Yoopers," which comes from U(pper) P(eninsula)-ERS.

The Upper Peninsula shares its western border with Wisconsin. To the east is Ontario, Canada. Lake Superior makes up its long, northern shore. To the south is Lake Michigan.

Pictured Rocks National Lakeshore shows the rocky and hilly nature of Michigan's Upper Peninsula.

Large deposits of copper and iron ore have been found in this region. There are also vast areas of forested land. Much of the western part of the region has rugged hills, including the Porcupine and Huron Mountains. The tallest point in Michigan is Mount Arvon. It rises up 1,979 feet (603 m) in the Huron Mountains.

The northernmost part of Michigan is Isle Royale, which is a large island in Lake Superior. A national park since 1940, it can only be visited by boat or floatplane.

CLIMATE AND WEATHER

Michigan has a continental climate, even though it is surrounded by the Great Lakes. Overall, it has hot, humid summers and cold, snowy winters. The average July high temperature is 80°F (27°C). The average January low is 12°F (-11°C). In the Upper Peninsula, summers are shorter, and winter temperatures are much colder.

Water evaporating from the Great Lakes causes many cloudy days. Thunderstorms rumble overhead about 30 days each year. Tornadoes can sometimes strike, especially in the Lower Peninsula. Twisters are rare in the Upper Peninsula.

In winter, the Upper Peninsula experiences huge amounts of lake-effect snow, thanks to evaporation from the Great Lakes. The city of Marquette averages more than 117 inches (297 cm) of snow yearly. Statewide, Michigan averages 33 inches (84 cm) of precipitation (both rain and snow) each year.

Severe storms can rip across the Great Lakes, endangering even the biggest freighters. In November 1975, the 729-foot (222-m) *Edmund Fitzgerald* was buffeted by a violent gale on Lake Superior as it was heading toward Detroit. The ship sank, dooming all 29 crewmembers.

PLANTS AND ANIMALS

Michigan has many kinds of plants and animals, thanks to its variety of habitats. Prairies, forests, shorelines, sand dunes, and wetlands can be found across the state.

In the early 1800s, nearly all of Michigan was forested. The state became a major supplier of lumber to the rest of the nation. Huge wooded areas were cut down. Some of those timberlands have since grown back. Today, about 19.3 million acres (7.8 million ha) of Michigan are covered in forests. That is 53 percent of the state's land area.

Much of the forestland in southern Michigan has been replaced by farmland and cities. In the Upper Peninsula, huge forests cover about 80 percent of the land.

A wide variety of plants and animals live in the state of Michigan. Sandhill cranes nest on the ground near or over shallow water in Michigan's marshes and bogs.

Ferns and moss grow near a waterfall on Michigan's Upper Peninsula.

In the bogs and marshes of the Upper Peninsula are many species of ferns and mosses. In the western mountains are vast forests of northern hemlock. Other common trees native to Michigan include birch, pine, sugar maple, oak, and black spruce.

PLANTS AND ANIMALS

Black Bear

The official state tree of Michigan is the white pine. These trees can tower up to 150 feet (46 m) high and live longer than 400 years. The state flower is the apple blossom. Michigan is also famous for its orchards of cherry trees. Most are in the northern part of the state. Michigan is a leading supplier of sweet and tart cherries.

White-tailed deer are very common in Michigan. Other large mammals spotted in the state include black bears, wolves, elk, moose, cougars, red foxes, and coyotes. Smaller animals include badgers, shrews, moles, bats, and flying squirrels. Even though Michigan is often called "The Wolverine State," these large, aggressive members of the weasel family are rarely seen.

Short-Eared Owl

Michigan's forest habitats shelter many kinds of birds. Species commonly seen in the state include wild turkeys, mourning doves, goldfinches, ravens, pileated woodpeckers, and endangered Kirtland's warblers. The official state bird is the American robin. Raptors include osprey, bald eagles, peregrine falcons, and short-eared owls. Aquatic birds found along Michigan's lakeshores include sandhill cranes, black terns, sandpipers, trumpeter swans, and loons.

Fish found lurking in Michigan's many lakes and rivers include bluegill, brown trout, salmon, bass, muskellunge, northern pike, perch, sturgeon, and walleye. Lake sturgeon can grow to over 8 feet (2.4 m) in length, weigh up to 800 pounds (363 kg), and live up to 100 years.

HISTORY

The first French explorers arrived in today's Michigan in the early 1600s. Before that time, the land was settled by several Algonquian-speaking Native American tribes. The most numerous were the Chippewa (Ojibwe), Ottawa, and Potawatomi. They formed a confederation called the Council of the Three Fires. They banded together for defense and trade. Smaller tribes included the Mascouten, Menominee, Miami, and the Saulk. The Huron (Wyandot) people were an Iroquoian-language people who also lived in the area.

From 1618-1622, Frenchman Étienne Brulé explored much of the Great Lakes region, including Michigan. He discovered that the area was filled with fur-bearing animals like beavers and foxes. Soon, French *voyageurs* were paddling canoes loaded with furs up and down Michigan's waterways. Fur trading made many people rich. Beaver pelts were prized in Europe for making hats.

A beaver pelt is stretched as it was by early fur traders.

French adventurer Antoine de la Mothe Cadillac landed in Detroit in 1701 with 100 men, including his young son and two missionaries.

Fur-trading centers sprang up all over the region. In 1668, French missionary Jacques Marquette founded Sault Ste. Marie in northeastern Michigan. In 1701, French adventurer Antoine de la Mothe Cadillac built Fort Pontchartrain du Détroit, which eventually became the city of Detroit. Fort Michilimackinac was built in 1715 along the important Straits of Mackinac, which connects Lake Huron and Lake Michigan.

Fur trading was so important in Michigan that European nations, especially France and Great Britain, went to war over control of the trapping grounds and trade routes. In the mid-1600s, even the Native Americans fought amongst themselves over the fur trade. The decades-long Iroquois Wars—also called the Beaver Wars—was one of the bloodiest conflicts ever fought in North America.

The 13 American colonies won freedom from Great Britain after the American Revolution (1775-1783). In 1787, Michigan became part of the Northwest Territory of the United States. Even after the war, the young United States and Great Britain clashed because of the fur trade. Michigan's boundaries were finally settled by the mid-1800s.

Native Americans bring furs to a ship to trade with Europeans.

A huge load of logs on a skidder in Michigan in the 1880s.

In 1805, Michigan Territory was formed. Settlement was slow until the Erie Canal opened in 1825. The waterway made it easier for people and goods to travel across New York State to the Great Lakes region. Many farms sprang up, and lumber and iron ore were shipped to big eastern cities.

On January 26, 1837, Michigan was finally admitted as the 26th state in the Union. Stevens Mason was elected as the state's first governor at just 24 years of age. He became the youngest governor in American history. The state capital moved from Detroit to Lansing in 1847. Lansing was more centrally located.

Michigan was strongly anti-slavery. Many runaway slaves were helped by the Underground Railroad in the state. Sojourner Truth was a freed slave and abolitionist. After moving to Michigan in 1857, she gave many public speeches about slavery, prison reform, and women's rights.

Sojourner Truth

In 1861, the country was engulfed by the Civil War (1861-1865). Michigan supported the Union with more than 90,000 troops to fight the Southern Confederacy. That was almost 25 percent of the male population of the state at that time. In 1863, Brigadier General George Custer led the Michigan Cavalry Brigade at the Battle of Gettysburg, in Pennsylvania. Leading his men into battle, Custer famously cried out, "Come on, you Wolverines!" They saved many Union lives by stopping a Confederate attack.

Brigadier General George Custer led the Michigan Cavalry Brigade at the Battle of Gettysburg. Custer's shout, "Come on, you Wolverines!" became their battle cry.

A General Motors auto assembly line in 1922.

After the Civil War and moving into the 20th century, Michigan's farms and industries continued to grow. Huge loads of copper, iron ore, and lumber were transported by ships and railroads. New industries emerged, such as furniture making and food processing. Detroit became a center for making automobiles.

In modern times, Michigan has been buffeted by severe economic downturns. The population has declined as jobs have dried up, especially in industrial cities like Detroit and Flint. The state is working hard to attract new employment opportunities, such as high-technology and renewable-energy businesses. The rebuilding of the state continues while Michigan looks to the future.

DID YOU KNOW?

• Michigan has more lighthouses than any other state, thanks to its 3,224 miles (5,189 km) of shoreline. The state's 129 lighthouses were built to guide ships through the often-stormy waters of the Great Lakes. While some are still lit each night, others have been closed because of modern ship navigation equipment, like GPS mapping. Many lighthouses have been converted to museums or bed-and-breakfast businesses. Copper Harbor Lighthouse on Lake Superior was built in 1866. Now fully restored, the lighthouse features a maritime museum, shipwreck artifacts, and walking paths.

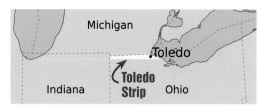

• Michigan is often called "The Wolverine State." From 1835-1836, the state almost got into a war with Ohio, its neighbor to the south. Their argument was over a narrow piece of land bordering the two states called the Toledo Strip. War was narrowly avoided. Ohio was given the Toledo Strip. In a compromise, Michigan took control of the resource-rich Upper Peninsula. Even though the issue was settled peacefully, the people of Ohio thought the Michiganders were as ornery as wolverines. The name stuck.

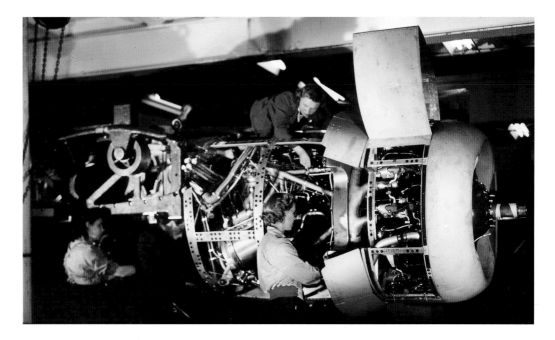

- During World War II (1939-1945), the United States needed war machines, especially airplanes, and it needed them quickly. The first factory to build aircraft on an assembly-line system was created in Michigan in 1942. Automaker Henry Ford used his experience with mass production to build the Willow Run bomber plant near Ypsilanti, Michigan. It was a 3.5-million-square-foot (325,161-sq-m) airplane factory designed to make B-24 Liberator bombers. The four-engine aircraft's long range and heavy bombing load made it effective in attacking targets in both Germany and Japan. At its peak, the Willow Run plant employed 42,000 workers. Many were women, who were collectively nicknamed "Rosie the Riveter." Before Willow Run, it took about a day to build a B-24 from the ground up. Willow Run's assembly line produced an aircraft *every hour*. Famous aviator Charles Lindbergh helped design the factory. He called Willow Run the "Grand Canyon of the Mechanized World." By the end of the war in 1945, Willow Run had built more than 8,600 B-24 Liberator bombers.

PEOPLE

Henry Ford (1863-1947) founded the Ford Motor Company in 1903. In his factories, he used mass production and assembly lines to build cars quickly and cheaply. This resulted in automobiles that were affordable for many middle-class Americans. Ford also believed in paying his workers high wages so they could afford to own a car themselves. The Ford Model T was introduced in 1908, selling for $825. Thanks to the efficient assembly lines, by 1916 the price had dropped to $360. The car came in one color. Ford famously said, "Any customer can have a car painted any color that he wants, so long as it is black." By the end of production in 1927, Ford sold more than 15 million Model Ts. Ford was born in Greenfield Township, Michigan.

Will Keith (W.K.) Kellogg (1860-1951) was born and raised in Battle Creek, Michigan. He and his brother, Dr. John Harvey Kellogg, operated a sanitarium, a health facility where sick people could heal. The Kellogg brothers were believers in healthy nutrition. They especially encouraged people to eat fruits, vegetables, and whole grains. In 1894, they invented a way of turning a mash of cereal grains into dough that could be cooked. It was then turned into delicious flakes. W.K. started his own cereal company in 1906 called the Battle Creek Toasted Corn Flake Company, which later became the Kellogg Company. Kellogg's Corn Flakes were a big success. In 1930, W.K. used his wealth to help people by creating the W.K. Kellogg Foundation, which gave away millions of dollars to charity.

Gerald Ford (1913-2006) was president of the United States from 1974-1977. He grew up in Grand Rapids. He was an Eagle Scout and a star football player for the University of Michigan. He was a congressman representing Michigan for 25 years. In 1973, he was appointed vice president by President Richard Nixon. When Nixon resigned the following year, Ford became president.

Diana Ross (1944-) is a singer, songwriter, and actress from Detroit. She was the lead singer of the vocal group The Supremes during the 1960s and 1970s. They recorded many hit records. The Supremes became the most successful group of Detroit's legendary Motown Records recording company. Ross then went on to a successful solo career. Her musical style includes rhythm & blues, soul, pop, and jazz. She won a Grammy Lifetime Achievement Award in 2012.

Taylor Lautner (1992-) is an actor best known for playing Jacob Black in *The Twilight Saga* film series, based on the novels by Stephenie Meyer. Lautner was born and grew up in Grand Rapids. He was a world champion martial artist before becoming an actor. His big break came in 2008 with the *Twilight* role of Jacob. In 2010, he was one of the highest paid teen actors in the country.

Madonna (1958-) is a singer, songwriter, actress, and record producer. She has sold more than 300 million records worldwide, making her one of the best-selling female recording artists of all time. Born in Bay City, Michigan, her real name is Madonna Louise Ciccone. Her pop music often causes controversy, but she has been a strong influence on many other artists. Madonna was inducted into the Rock and Roll Hall of Fame in 2008.

CITIES

Detroit is the largest city in Michigan. Its population is 680,250. Together with its suburbs and surrounding cities—like Ann Arbor and Flint—it is home to more than 5 million people. The city began in 1701 as a fur-trading post on the shores of the Detroit River. In the early 1900s, so many automobile factories sprang up that Detroit became known as the "Motor City," or "Motown." Ford, Chrysler, and General Motors are major area employers. Construction, finance, health care, and information technology are also important. In recent years, due to America's declining automobile industry, Detroit has gone through tough times. It is working hard to grow businesses and attract new residents.

Grand Rapids, Michigan

Gerald R. Ford Presidential Museum

Meijer Gardens & Sculpture Park

Grand Rapids is Michigan's second-largest city. Its population is 193,792. It is located along the Grand River in the southwestern part of the Lower Peninsula, close to Lake Michigan. Its nickname is "Furniture City." In the city's early days, logs shipped down the Grand River were used to make wood products, including fine furniture. Several office furniture companies continue to make Grand Rapids their headquarters. Other big employers include health care, publishing, insurance, plus automotive and aviation manufacturing. There are several colleges and universities in the city. Grand Rapids is also home to the Gerald R. Ford Presidential Museum, the John Ball Zoo, and the Frederik Meijer Gardens & Sculpture Park.

Lansing became the capital of Michigan in 1847. Its population is 114,620. It is located in the south-central part of the

Lower Peninsula. The biggest employers are government, education, health care, life insurance, and manufacturing. Lansing is also home to Michigan State University, one of the top public universities in the country. The top-rated R.E. Olds Transportation Museum has dozens of classic Oldsmobile automobiles in its permanent collection.

Kalamazoo is in the southwestern corner of Michigan's Lower Peninsula. Its population is 75,922. There are several pharmaceutical

and medical device manufacturers in the city. Western Michigan University and Kalamazoo College make their home in Kalamazoo. The Kalamazoo Air Zoo is a museum featuring 50 rare and historical aircraft, including an SR-71B Blackbird, the fastest airplane ever built.

Sault Ste. Marie is located by the rapids of the St. Marys River. It is on the far eastern end of the Upper Peninsula, across the river from Ontario, Canada. Founded in 1668, it is Michigan's oldest city. Today, its population is 13,959. The Soo Locks allow massive 1,000-foot (305-m) freighters carrying coal, iron ore, and grain to bypass the rapids and move between Lake Superior and Lake Huron. Part of the St. Lawrence Seaway, the locks handle nearly 7,000 ships each year.

Marquette is the largest city on Michigan's Upper Peninsula. Its population is 21,441. The Northern Michigan University Wildcats play in the city's Superior Dome. At 14 stories tall, it is the world's largest wooden dome, with a seating capacity of 8,000. Marquette is an active Lake Superior shipping port. Giant freighters load up with iron ore pellets, called taconite, at the city's Presque Isle Harbor.

TRANSPORTATION

The Great Lakes and connecting waterways have always been important for transporting cargo and people, from the days of birchbark canoes to modern 1,000-foot (305-m) -long freighters. During the busy summer shipping season, thousands of vessels each year pass through the Soo Locks in Sault Ste. Marie and the Detroit River.

The Mackinac Bridge connects the Upper and Lower Peninsulas. It was built in 1957. The suspension bridge runs 5 miles (8 km) across the Straits of Mackinac. Before it was constructed, ferries shuttled people and cars across the waterway.

Michigan is famous for building automobiles. Naturally, there are many roads and highways that crisscross the state. Interstates I-69 and I-75 run generally north and south, while I-94 and I-96 run east and west. In total, Michigan has 122,141 miles (196,567 km) of public roadways.

The Mackinac Bridge is 5 miles (8 km) long.

Michigan has 27 railroads hauling freight on 3,542 miles (5,700 km) of track across the state. Coal, automobiles, metallic ores, and farm products are the most common products carried by rail. Amtrak also carries passengers between several Michigan cities and Chicago, Illinois.

Detroit Metropolitan Wayne County Airport is Michigan's busiest airport. It handles about 33 million passengers each year. Other airports include the Gerald R. Ford International Airport in Grand Rapids, and Flint Bishop International Airport in Flint.

Detroit Metropolitan Wayne County Airport

NATURAL
RESOURCES

Most of Michigan's 51,600 farms are located in the southern part of the state. The soil and climate there are more favorable for growing crops. Michigan's farms create almost $9 billion in business each year. The most valuable products are dairy, corn, and soybeans. The state is also a top producer of cherries, apples, blueberries, and squash. Large numbers of flowers and plants are also grown in Michigan, including begonias, Easter lilies, tulips, and petunias.

A woman picks blueberries at a farm in Covert, Michigan.

Pine logs from Michigan's Upper Peninsula await loading onto a train.

In the late 1800s, Michigan was the top producer of pine lumber. By 1900, much of the state's forests had been chopped down, marking an end to the lumber boom. Today, many trees have regrown, and the lumber industry practices better forest conservation. Michigan has about 20 million acres (8.1 million ha) of forestland. Most logging takes place in the Upper Peninsula and the northern half of the Lower Peninsula. The most common trees logged are maple, oak, and pine. The industry employs more than 27,000 people and produces $8.1 billion in business. Michigan is one of the top producers of Christmas trees.

Native Americans mined copper in Michigan's Upper Peninsula almost 5,000 years ago. In the late 1800s, Michigan led the nation in copper mining, but deep-shaft mining grew too expensive. Most copper mines closed. Today, Michigan's most important mining products include iron ore, limestone, gypsum, plus sand and gravel.

NATURAL RESOURCES

INDUSTRY

Detroit is called "Motor City" for good reason: General Motors, Ford, and Chrysler all have their headquarters in or near the city. Michigan is the top automobile manufacturer in the United States. In 2014, more than 2.3 million cars and trucks rolled off assembly lines in Michigan. There are also more than 1,700 auto-related manufacturing businesses. The industry supports tens of thousand of jobs, many of which require advanced skills. More than 89,000 engineers are employed in Michigan, a higher concentration than anywhere else in the country.

Because Michigan is so heavily invested in car making, the state's economy rises and falls with the industry. In recent decades, severe recessions and fierce competition from foreign companies have hurt Michigan. However, the industry is bouncing back. The state's car companies are investing in factories, building research-and-development centers, and creating thousands of new jobs.

A new vehicle is tested at a General Motors Assembly Plant in Lansing, Michigan. GM plants produce several brands of cars, including Chevrolets, Buicks, and Cadillacs.

Boxes of Kellogg's Corn Flakes move across a conveyor belt at a manufacturing plant in Battle Creek, Michigan. Battle Creek is nicknamed "Cereal City" because the Kellogg Company and Post Cereal were founded there.

Other important industries in Michigan include food products, aerospace, furniture, military equipment, and information technology. Battle Creek is nicknamed "Cereal City." Both the Kellogg Company and Post Cereal were founded in Battle Creek, makers of such breakfast favorites as Kellogg's Corn Flakes and Raisin Bran, and Post's Honeycomb.

Michigan is becoming a favorite year-round vacation destination. Tourism is a big part of the state's economy. More than 113 million people visit Michigan each year, spending more than $22.8 billion and creating 214,000 jobs.

SPORTS

Michigan has several professional major league sports teams. All are based in the Detroit area. The Detroit Lions are in the National Football League. They play in Detroit's Ford Field. The Detroit Tigers play in Major League Baseball's American League. Founded in 1894, the team has won four World Series titles.

The Detroit Red Wings compete in the National Hockey League, one of the NHL's original six teams. Founded in 1926, the Red Wings have won 11 Stanley Cup championships, more than any other American team. The Detroit Pistons play in the National Basketball Association. Since moving to Detroit from Indiana in 1957, the Pistons have won three NBA championship titles.

University of Michigan Wolverines play out of Ann Arbor, Michigan.

Sparty the Spartan is the mascot for East Lansing's Michigan State University.

College sports are very popular in Michigan. The University of Michigan at Ann Arbor has 27 varsity teams dubbed the Wolverines. The football team plays in a massive outdoor stadium nicknamed "The Big House." The Spartans represent Michigan State University in East Lansing. The football, basketball, hockey, and golf teams have won many national titles.

Because of Michigan's vast forests, many parks, and seemingly endless miles of beaches, the state is a favorite among campers, hikers, anglers, bikers, and hunters.

Water sports are a big part of Michigan's sports scene, thanks to more than 11,000 inland lakes, and 36,000 miles (57,936 km) of rivers and streams, plus four Great Lakes. Popular activities include sailing, kayaking, fishing, and scuba diving.

ENTERTAINMENT

Detroit is nicknamed "Motor City," or "Motown." But Motown also stands for Motown Records, a famous record company that made it big in the 1960s. The label specialized in soul-pop music. It launched many superstar acts, including The Supremes, Smokey Robinson, Stevie Wonder, the Jackson 5, and Marvin Gaye. Music continues to be a big part of Detroit's cultural scene. The city is home to the Detroit Symphony Orchestra.

The Gilmore Car Museum in Hickory Corners displays hundreds of vintage automobiles, including a 1927 Ford Model T and a 1913 Rolls-Royce. For car buyers, the North American International Auto Show has been held in Detroit almost every year since 1907.

The Fox Theatre in Detroit is a National Historic Landmark. Opened in 1928, the ornate venue seats more than 5,000 and hosts live performances by some of the biggest names in show business.

The Gilmore Car Museum features hundreds of vintage cars, including a 1930 Rolls-Royce Sedanca Deville used in the 1967 Walt Disney film The Gnome-Mobile.

Mackinac Island is a popular vacation destination where no cars are allowed.

The Gerald R. Ford Presidential Museum is located at the University of Michigan in Grand Rapids. It preserves thousands of documents and artifacts from the life of the 38th president of the United States.

For nature and history lovers, Mackinac Island is a large resort island on Lake Huron, near the Straits of Mackinac. It was first settled as a mission, fur-trading post, and fort. Today, there are many historical buildings, art galleries, and festivals. The island can only be reached by boat or small aircraft.

ENTERTAINMENT

TIMELINE

1000 AD—Chippewa (Ojibwe), Ottawa, and Potawatomi tribes settle into the Michigan area.

1618—Frenchman Étienne Brulé begins exploring the Great Lakes region.

1701—French adventurer Antoine de la Mothe Cadillac builds a fort that eventually becomes the city of Detroit.

1715—Fort Michilimackinac built along the Straits of Mackinac between Lake Huron and Lake Michigan.

1805—Michigan Territory is formed, becoming a territory of the United States.

1836—The Toledo War, a territorial conflict between Ohio and Michigan, is resolved.

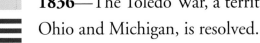

1837—Michigan becomes the 26th state.

1847—Lansing replaces Detroit as the capital of Michigan.

1855—The Soo Locks open at Sault Ste. Marie.

1861-65—Michigan sends 90,000 troops to serve in the Union army.

1888—Michigan's lumber production peaks.

1908—Ford introduces the Model T automobile.

1941-45—During World War II, Michigan companies build military weapons and vehicles. Detroit is nicknamed the Arsenal of Democracy.

1957—The Mackinac Bridge is completed, connecting the Lower and Upper Peninsulas.

2008—Detroit Red Wings win the Stanley Cup.

2012—General Motors reports record profits, signaling the beginning of a turnaround for the troubled Michigan automotive industry.

2015—High levels of lead are found in the blood of Flint, Michigan, children after the city botches the switch to a new water system while trying to cut costs. High levels of lead can cause irreversible brain damage in children.

GLOSSARY

American Revolution

The war fought between the American colonies and Great Britain from 1775-1783. It is also known as the War of Independence or the Revolutionary War.

Assembly Line

A way of manufacturing goods in which parts are added to a semi-finished product as it moves from station to station. Many workers are used to complete a product, but each worker is responsible for just one part or section. By specializing the process, goods can be made rapidly and efficiently.

Civil War

The war fought between America's Northern and Southern states from 1861-1865. The Southern states were for slavery. They wanted to start their own country. Northern states fought against slavery and a division of the country.

Erie Canal

A 360-mile (579-km) -long waterway running across New York state to Lake Erie. Opened in 1825, people and supplies could then be transported inland. This greatly helped with the settlement of the American Midwest.

Gale

A very strong wind, often accompanied by a storm.

Glacier

Huge, slow-moving sheets of ice that grow and shrink as the climate changes. During the Ice Age, some glaciers covered entire regions and measured more than one mile (1.6 km) thick.

Lake Effect Snow

Winter weather systems often pick up huge amounts of evaporated water as they pass over the Great Lakes. Once over cold land, the moisture condenses and falls as heavy snow, sometimes as far as 20 miles (32 km) inland.

Mission

A large building or fort that Christians used as a base to spread their religion to the local people.

Motown

Both a nickname for Detroit (Motor Town) and a style of rhythm-and-blues music developed in the city. Motown Records launched many superstar acts in the 1960s while headquartered in Detroit.

St. Lawrence Seaway

A waterway between the United States and Canada that allows ships to travel from the Atlantic Ocean to the Great Lakes.

Underground Railroad

In the early- to mid-1800s, people created the Underground Railroad to help African Americans escape from slave states. Not an actual railroad, it was instead a secret network of safe houses and connecting routes that led slaves to freedom.

Voyageur

French Canadian workers who paddled canoes laden with furs in the 18th and 19th centuries. They paddled long distances through wilderness areas, mainly in Canada and the upper Midwest. Voyageur is a French word that means "traveler."

INDEX